What Is Important?
What Is Important!

John DeCotis

ISBN 978-1-64191-244-0 (paperback)
ISBN 978-1-64191-245-7 (digital)

Christian Faith Publishing, Inc.
832 Park Avenue
Meadville, PA 16335
www.christianfaithpublishing.com

Printed in the United States of America

To my wife, my inspiration, a true person of faith, my children, my grandchildren, my extended family, and my parents who instilled their faith in me.

FOREWORD

I am a former religious education teacher, school teacher, school administrator, education executive, community volunteer, husband, father, grandfather and an active church member among many other things. I live in Fayetteville, Georgia, and am lucky to live in a community with many churches and people whom live out their faith.

I have written this piece to explore, discuss, and answer many of the questions I received as a religious education teacher. Also, many of these questions have arisen in my many other roles and activities from people whom I engage with every day. Some of the questions have originated with me from my many experiences, readings, and research into questions I receive from others.

The answers given are based on some church doctrine, the Bible, research, personal experiences, and the experiences of others.

I hope this piece offers some a direction and some comfort for those who are questioning their faith or are just looking for answers to their questions to complicated and sometimes contradictory information.

CHAPTER 1

In the accelerated and often chaotic lifestyle characteristic of our current times, we all need to step back and determine what is important.

Throughout history and during our current everyday lives, we have had many opportunities and challenges. These challenges confront our institutions, our families, and us as individuals. As people of religious faith, what is our plan? Do we carry on along our current path? Do we change our behaviors or foster change amongst others? In this work, we will explore these and many other issues that you may have to encounter or respond to as you stretch your faith, put it into perspective, and make it a positive force in your sphere of influence.

The first thing each of us needs to do is determine our faith. To do this, we need to ask ourselves many relevant questions.

What do we believe?

Why do we believe what we do?

Who has influenced these beliefs?

Are we comfortable with our beliefs faced with conflicting empirical evidence?

How often do we question our beliefs?

How often do we discuss our faith?

Do we see contradictions and hypocritical threads in our beliefs?

Do we truly understand where we stand in the big picture?

We will explore these questions and others as we begin to assess our standing with God and the current status of our *faith*. As we do this, it is important to not judge the position or beliefs of others, but rather to assess our own beliefs and determine where we are.

What do we believe?

In answering the question, "What do we believe?," it is important to determine the context of the question. Are we comparing what we believe to what others believe? Are we comparing what we believe to the teachings of Christianity? Are we comparing what we believe to the norm in our society? Of course, we are comparing what we believe to these and much more.

Did you ever think about how your actions reflect what you really believe, not what you purport to believe? For example, do you have empathy for the poor, for the sick, for the disadvantaged, but never take any action to help? Do you ask God to forgive you, but you do not forgive others? So our first step is to determine if our thoughts and actions are consistent. We can do this by writing down a few statements outlining what we think we believe. For example, a few of these could be:

"I believe everyone is equal."

"I believe in free speech."

"I believe in the power of the Holy Spirit."

Now next to each statement, write down some instances of your behavior that either support or do not support these beliefs. How did you do?

Why do we believe what we believe?

Once we know if our beliefs and behaviors are consistent, we can try to determine why be believe what we believe. Most of what people believe is learned behavior. These behaviors can be taught to you through either personal experiences or someone teaching you and modeling for you. When you are developing your beliefs for the most part, this is happening without you being conscious of it.

Therefore, our first step is to write down some memories. Memories that conjure up emotions are usually those that establish a belief. For instance, if a mean dog knocks you down when you are a small child and scares you, you may believe that all dogs are mean. If your parent emotionally talks in a negative way about a specific group of people, then you may establish negative beliefs about that group.

Once you write down these memories, try to determine what your current beliefs are concerning those experiences. This will give you a good idea where you are in terms of why you may believe certain things.

Who has influenced these beliefs?

When looking at your beliefs, it is important to note who has influenced these beliefs. This will give you guidance in determining the real value and authenticity of these beliefs. For example, you may value education. You may believe that a good education is necessary. Your parents also believe in the value of a good education. It is reasonable to determine that your parents influenced this belief in you. Your parents believe it is wrong to steal from someone. However, you believe stealing is justified under certain circumstances. It is obvious you did not learn this behavior from your parents. Therefore, it is necessary to evaluate those who may have influenced this behavior (friends, neighbors, relatives, teachers, etc.).

By questioning and determining who may have influenced certain beliefs you may have, this can help you assess the legitimacy of these beliefs and impact your future behaviors.

Are we comfortable with our beliefs faced with conflicting empirical evidence?

Sometimes, we are not always sure of what we believe until confronted with a situation where we have to act on these beliefs. For instance, you may not support gambling or lotteries. However, you may send your child to a lottery-supported preschool. Then you realize, maybe I do support gambling after all.

When this occurs, how do you react? Do you consciously change your stance or your beliefs? Do your actions continue to contradict your purported beliefs? These are questions that are difficult to answer. When your beliefs as a Christian and your behaviors are not consistent, do those around you ever accuse you of being a hypocrite? If so, then you probably will not be comfortable. This is the time to take a stand and measure your true status.

How often do we question our beliefs?

As people of *faith*, it is important to know where we stand and to stand there! Faith sometimes is clear and sometimes it is foggy.

Sometimes, we know the answer; sometimes, we seek the answer. Therefore, it is important to think about our beliefs, challenge our beliefs, and hold true to our beliefs. It is not unusual for people to question their faith, especially during difficult times. When this occurs, it is necessary to stay true to your faith and through the Holy Spirit, to force your difficult challenge, to work hard to disprove your beliefs. Faith is not quantifiable, proved and disproved through science and logic.

For example, you apply for your dream job. You pray to the Lord to help you get this job. Someone else gets the job. Do you question your faith? Do you deny the Lord since you put him to the test? How often does this happen? Keep a tabulation of when you think you have questioned your beliefs. This will give you an indication of your commitment to your beliefs.

How often do we discuss our faith?

When we discuss our faith with others, this shows we are confident in our faith and beliefs. Do we do this often? When we do, in what type of setting does this take place? Some people are reluctant to discuss their faith because they do not want to appear pushy or they do not want to offend anyone. However, one can discuss their faith without doing either of these things. Talking about your faith is important because it affirms your beliefs. It also shows that your actions and behaviors (we hope so) are based on your strong Christian faith.

The best way to talk about your faith is to integrate it into everyday conversation, not to bring it on as a speech or an argument to try to change someone's behavior. For example, you are with a group of friends and you are discussing how someone has wronged all of you and some in the group want revenge. As a Christian, this would be a good time to bring up reasons why revenge is wrong and offer forgiveness instead citing examples from Christ and his apostles. Another example is when someone you know complains that their best friend has abandoned them because they are going through a personal crisis. This crisis has resulted in them acting immorally and irrationally. They are ready to ignore and dump this friend because they feel offended and ignored. This is an opportunity for you to cite the importance for Christians to forgive this type of behavior and to help this friend in need as is Christ's way. Another example is to demonstrate your faith by performing an action and citing why you did this. Let's say you volunteer at a homeless shelter, and you see a man needs a coat. You give this man the coat off your back and refer back to what Jesus and his apostles had to say about helping the poor among us.

All of these examples are good ways to talk about your faith without making people defensive and hardening their hearts.

Do we truly understand where we stand in the big picture?

This question had been contemplated by people for centuries! By assessing your beliefs, where they come from and how you put them into practice, this will give you some indication. If you are a person of faith, you know you have a place and your life has meaning. With this in mind, you cannot only help to control your own destiny, but also help others control theirs. In this next section, we will look at the various ways that you can determine for yourself what is important and help others to do the same.

CHAPTER 2

Making Determinations

So you know what it is all about! Are you sure? Let us take some time to explore what it means to be a Christian. Here are some questions we need to explore:

Do you regularly go to church?

Do you put into practice what Christ preaches?

How do you interact with others?

Is Christ a part of your everyday activities?

Do you regularly go to church?

Does going to church determine if you are a good Christian? The answer to this is probably not. However, if you do go to church regularly, you are better engaged in the work of the "body of Christ" or the Church community as a whole. This enables you to fulfill many of the gospels by participating in Christian-centered services to others. Also, by going to church regularly, you stay connected to Christ and the Holy Spirit by participating in the sacraments and by staying in close touch with the Christian community. Consequently, you can be a good Christian in terms of your beliefs without going to church regularly, but you will find it hard to maximize your potential as a Christian and fulfill your obligations.

Do you put into practice what Christ preaches?

This is a difficult task for most people. Many of the teachings of Christ are contrary to things of this world. We are asked to do things that oftentimes go against our human nature. Therefore, if you feel that you are struggling, remember you are not alone. The challenge here is to be the best Christian you can be on a daily basis.

One suggestion to measure your status is to give yourself the "Three Strike Test" daily.

Did you forgive anyone today?

Did you deny the Lord today?

Did you throw the first stone today?

Did you forgive anyone today?

Every day as a Christian is a struggle. We encounter people, places, and circumstances that place us at odds with other people. Sometimes, they or we can be unreasonable, inconsiderate, and outright mean.

When we find ourselves in this position, how do we handle it? Do we hold grudges for many years? Do we try to get back at people? Do try to place ourselves in a position where we avoid a person, place. or thing? If so, we must try very hard to forgive. This is not always natural or desirable, but it is the Christian thing to do. Throughout the Bible and Christian teachings, we hear time and time again that Jesus forgives those that transgress him. In fact, while on his cross, he forgives those that crucified him and a criminal hanging next to him. He also asks us to forgive over and over again and cites many examples as to how this can be done. He also demonstrates this to his apostles on numerous occasions.

So we ask ourselves, as Christians, did we forgive anyone today? If not, it is time to get started. Let us then start tomorrow and keep tabs from now on.

Did you deny the Lord today?

What does this mean? In a nutshell, it means that the cock crowed three times on us! Yes, we denied the Lord. We questioned him as the people questioned Moses and challenged the Lord when they were lost in the desert for forty years. We put him to the test. We doubted him. If we are believers, how does this happen? It happens because we are human. We are self-centered. Sometimes. we think the Lord only thinks about us. Something bad happens to us and we think we are abandoned. We try hard for a promotion and we do not get it. We ask the Lord, "Why not?" I deserve this! We pray hard for something and it does not happen. We ask the Lord, "Why did you not listen to me?" The Lord listens and in fact knows all. He has a grand plan that we do not know or understand. Sometimes, when the Lord is listening to us. he gives us hints and answers as to what our actions may be. These could be an insight, another person's advice, a revelation, or even actions by others that move us in the right direction. Prayers are answered in mysterious and indirect ways according to his plan.

Our goal should be to look for these signs and keep the faith; they are sometimes right in front of our eyes. To gauge yourself, take the time to note when you lose the faith. Then pray and meditate on what signs can I find around me. I am sure you will find many.

Did you throw the first stone today?

Judging is something that is reserved to the Lord not us. Yes, we do this all the time. We again are human with our own thoughts and values. We judge others to be good or bad, better or worse, and a number of other ways. When we judge, we throw the first stone for we are forgetting that we are not without sin. How often do we ignore others or write them off because we deem them to be unworthy of our attention? Adolescents do this to their parents because they judge them to be old and out of touch.

Politicians do this to their opponents and often to some of their constituents if they have a different philosophy or point of view.

To avoid judging and condemning, we must first forgive, then seek to understand. Once we do this. we will be able to agree to disagree.

How did you do with the "Three Strike Test?" Did you strike out? If so, you need batting practice. Be cognizant of how you do each day and practice on getting a hit or a home run!

CHAPTER 3

How does our faith enable us to cope with other religions, cultures and faith? In this Chapter we will explore this and several other questions.

What about other religions?

Who is right and who is wrong? Wars are fought over this and have been for ages. How do we know what is legitimate and what is not? Are other religions and philosophies equal to our own as Christians? The answer to this question is a resounding NO! As Christians, if we follow the word of God as it is presented in the Bible, then we are on the right track to salvation. So what do all of these other religions, philosophies, and beliefs mean? To make a long story short, Abraham is the foundation for Judaism, Christianity, and Islam. His belief in God and in the word of the Lord permeates throughout these religions. However, only through Christianity is the true path to salvation realized through Jesus Christ. What then happens to these believers in other faiths? What about atheists and nonbelievers? What about those that intentionally believe in and worship the devil?

What happens to believers in other faiths?

As we know, God is omnipotent. He knows the hearts of all men and women. Through the intervention of the Holy Spirit, God will judge all men and women on their final day. This mystery is not for us to judge or figure out but to accept.

What about nonbelievers?

Nonbelievers choose to make a decision, "Not to believe." This is a more difficult situation to rectify, especially since people have God's gift of "free will." However, if they reconcile and have a spark of "belief and faith'," then the Lord through the assistance of the Holy Spirit will have to judge the status of this person.

Nonbelievers are "separated" from God, and only God can judge whether this separation has ended. If separation from God does not end, then condemnation is at risk.

What about those that intentionally believe in and worship the devil?

These folks have made a conscious decision to accept the evil of the devil and every false promise he makes. They are totally separated from God and even contrary to God. Again, it will take reconciliation and a relationship with God to change their status. God forgives infinitely more than 77and always leaves the door open for those that repent. If one fails to repent, then the devil will have his prize.

CHAPTER 4

As a Christian, what is my mission and what should my actions be? To address this question, let us look at an example of a person we all may know.

Let us talk about Mr. Henry. Henry is a religious person. He goes to church on a regular basis. He believes in God and Jesus Christ the only Son of God. He goes about his daily business and doesn't bother anyone. He attends to his own business and does his job with diligence.

On the other hand, Henry misrepresents items on his income tax, is really not welcoming to others, and pays little attention to the needs of his family and those around him. What should his mission and actions be as a Christian?

As Christians, our mission should be to act as Christ would have us act. This means to share our grace and to offer others our faith, hope, and charity/love. These are gifts we receive from the Lord, and we need to make it our mission to share these gifts with others. Additionally, we as Christians receive the gifts of the Holy Spirit on a regular basis. Again, it should be our mission to share these with others. These gifts are many and are not always obvious for us to see, at least not right away!

What does this look like? Well, Henry should offer the gifts he has received to others. This will give them the opportunity to fully embrace everything that the Lord has to offer. As he deals with people on a "day-by-day" basis, he should offer hope through encouraging people when they are down, by sharing his faith through actions and witnessing when people appear lost and life has no meaning and love/charity by giving of himself to others when they need support, backup, and a friend.

Also, some actions would also include praying, giving of alms, service to the church/society, and tithing. Through conducting all four of these actions, you stay true to the Lord. and you fulfill your mission.

CHAPTER 5

In an increasing secular society, how do I hold to my beliefs and still live the word, but not turn away those who do not believe or practice their faith?

This becomes increasingly difficult as we encounter people every day who do not believe what we believe. However, as Christians, the expectation for us is to treat all people in a Christ-like manner. Through our actions and our words, we can show what Christianity is all about and win over people's hearts and minds. For those that are intentional about hurting us physically and or mentally, we should continue to treat them as a Christian is expected, but we need to be realistic about being proactive and take measures to keep ourselves safe. This means to give a helping hand, to encourage, and to give hope. This also means we go above and beyond to serve. This does not mean to let the person or group of people to harm us in any way.

Do we need to forgive and be forgiven to survive in a secular society?

Yes, the trademark of a Christian is to forgive and likewise to ask for forgiveness. This will cement our relationship with the Lord. While dying on his cross, the criminal next to Jesus asks for forgiveness and is granted eternal life. When someone does you wrong, to forgive them is to free them to seek forgiveness from God. Likewise, when you ask someone for forgiveness, it opens the door for your peace and to feel free when asking God for forgiveness. In a secular society, it is necessary to show our faith through forgiving and asking for forgiveness. This demonstrates the strength and truth of our beliefs as Christians.

What is the strength in a secular society?

This is a tough question. It depends on what we mean by a secular society. If we mean one that does not adopt a particular religion, then the strength is that we have the freedom to worship our true faith. If we mean a society that has no spirit, no rules, no conscience, or no values, then we have a problem. In a society such as this, it is necessary for our Christian community to serve as our society and to function as a part of our larger society. This will allow us to serve as Christians, but also to evangelize through our actions and words the larger society.

Why do societies become secular?

When a society becomes secular, it is usually the result of people feeling they do not need God or that God does not help them or anyone else when in need. Also, often people misunderstand science and believe that it has the answers that we seek. Sometimes, people just outright reject God since they are hardcore nonbelievers. Additionally, people in general may be confused, disheartened, and misled due to personal or worldly issues. Remember, the Lord never abandons us but rather lifts and carries us through difficult times.

If one studies science closely, it becomes apparent that science can explain some things, but not a majority. Science can sometimes prove or disprove, but only in very controlled and limited circumstances. When one has true faith, wisdom and answers are plentiful and fulfilling. Those without faith may see faith as a superstition or unsubstantiated, they feel they need proof. Unfortunately, faith and God are difficult to prove scientifically, but can be experienced. Once experienced, one becomes a believer.

How do you experience faith?

This is a highly personal experience! Some people experience faith through a feeling they get through prayer. Others through the feeling they get through service or being helped by others. Still, others experience faith through revelation or seeing/feeling something for the first time that has always been in their presence. Most of the time, experiencing faith is accompanied by a feeling. A feeling of warmth, comfort, presence, and even belongingness. Oftentimes, this experience of faith occurs as one of the many gifts of the Holy

Spirit. You will know it when you experience it. Seek to experience it, and then you will know you are one with God.

One you experience faith, you are now prepared to share this experience with others.

How do I share this experience with others?

The best way to share this experience is to describe it. Most people will be interested in hearing about it, especially if they are interested in the topic. However, describing it and telling about it are nothing compared to the actual experience. Once again, by living your faith, you offer a positive role model for your experience.

CHAPTER 6

How do we respond when people tell us that churches are full of hypocrites?

First and foremost, the world is full of hypocrites. All professions, all organizations, and yes, all churches have hypocrites. It is human nature to see the faults and inconsistencies in others and not ourselves.

Our goal in talking to others is to paint the picture of "How much worse things would be without churches!" Our goal as Christians and also as church attendees is to work on being consistent and not be hypocrites as much as possible. Will we ever reach this goal 100 percent? No, we will not! However, we should strive to do so. In other walks of life, others may not strive as hard as we do. When we are hypocritical, we must examine our actions and determine if they are consistent with our Christian beliefs. For example, do we purport to be Christian, but believe it is okay to steal from our boss? This and other questions must be honestly asked.

When we violate the rules of a church, what does this do to our relationship with God?

This all depends on the severity of the infraction. All churches do not have the same rules and obligations. When you decide to join a particular church, you agree to follow the rules of that church. This is in a sense is a contract. When you violate a rule, you need to reconcile with the church in which you belong.

How this impacts our relationship with God depends on the type and severity of the infraction. Questions you must ask yourself are the following: Is this an affront to God? Did I deny or challenge God? Does it violate the tenants of Christianity? Did I not love my neighbor or help those in need, or did I judge someone? Does it violate the Ten Commandments? Did I commit a breach of my contract with God? Have you sinned in the eyes of God?

In essence, when you violate a church rule, it may not be an affront to God. Keep tabs of this so you can reconcile with God when you violate his teachings.

How do we know if we are hypocrites?

Being a hypocrite is not a full-time job! Usually, this is situational. People act in a hypocritical manner because they do not truly fully understand what they really believe in general and they do not see themselves in the greater picture. For example, a person may believe it is wrong for their children to speak to them in a disrespectful manner. However, they speak to their children in a disrespectful manner. They may also say to their spouse, "Do not drive over the speed limit," while they drive over the speed limit all the time. Other times, they may preach honesty to their children and always demonstrate honesty. Therefore, being a hypocrite is usually not 100 percent of the time. Strive to be open minded and watch for when your actions and words are not true to your beliefs. Make of list of the pluses and minuses of your behaviors. When you see that you are not being true to yourself, make note of this and work on making every situation consistent.

CHAPTER 7

How do we work in a "dog-eat-dog" business or work environment and hold true to our Christian values and beliefs?

To survive in our competitive workplace and society, it is important to put things into perspective and to hold fast to your beliefs and values. The best way to get ahead is to be honest, dedicated, loyal, and hardworking. Trying to embarrass someone, undermine, or misrepresent will only catch up with you in the end. Likewise, positive supportive behaviors will only benefit you in the end. Your employer will be able to see through false and damaging behaviors. People talk and bosses observe. You may temporarily get ahead with unscrupulous behaviors, but not for long. In fact, some organizations welcome and highly reward honest character and Christian values such as Chick-fil-A and Hobby Lobby.

How do I pursue Christian actions where these values are not appreciated?

Always hold true to yourself. Oftentimes, it is difficult to refrain from acting like those around you. They may be unscrupulous, mean spirited, and unappreciative. However, they can never take away your faith. Sometimes, it is worth changing your environment to one where your values and beliefs are appreciated. From this vantage point, you can continue to share your good works within your environment to build community or outside of your environment to welcome new members into you community.

Do work environments have to be secular?

No, they do not. Most places allow people to wear religious metals, skullcaps, rings, etc. and display religious books or objects as long as they are not overpowering. Additionally, statements such as "God Bless You," "Thank God," or "You are in my prayers" are common and acceptable most of the time.

In the workplace, you have the opportunity to "act" like a Christian and display a servant attitude while providing a positive role model for others. This is how you can have the biggest impact while holding to your faith and values.

Are work and faith intertwined?

Yes, absolutely, when you speak on the phone, when you write a report, when you interact with clients or co-workers, and when you work diligently on your own. Everything you do should reflect your faith. When you are a believer in God and the living Christ, your actions and words should reflect this in every setting. If not, then this should be a goal of yours. A little reflection and intentional action on your part will enable you to hold true to your faith.

CHAPTER 8

Truth and Faith

How do I explain God, church, and faith to children?

This can sometimes be tricky and difficult. Always start by being a mirror of your faith. Be a good role model. Children will pick up on your nonverbal behavior quickly. Always treat the children with dignity and respect as you teach them the word. Use real-life examples to get you point across, using current times and places. Be honest and do not have an answer for everything! We know that faith is infinite in its wisdom and this is based on true understanding not hard, cold facts. Our Christian beliefs have several mysteries that we know are true but hard to prove scientifically. Children will accept mysteries such as the resurrection, the consecration, the virgin birth, and many others when presented honestly by a person of true faith.

What is the truth?

This question has been debated throughout history. People can make all kinds of arguments on this issue. However, there is only one irrefutable answer. Truth is the wisdom that is in the Bible. At first glance and even with a first reading, the wisdom of the Bible does not jump out to you. It is only after several readings and reflection do you begin to see it. This truth becomes even more obvious as you see it in relation to your everyday experiences. When you feel and experience the things that you read in the Bible, they become more meaningful and you see the light. For example, when you read the Beatitudes, it is difficult to understand them unless you experience them. (Blessed are the mourners for they will be comforted.) When someone close to you dies, this comes to light.

Truth is in the Bible. Read, reflect, and open your heart, and you will see this!

How do I share the truth with others?

It is not worthwhile, and it is counterproductive to argue with someone who is without faith about truth. Is their truth the same as yours, "tit for tat?" Instead hold true to the wisdom and truth that comes from scripture. Your modeling and example will help promote the "truth." Also, ensure that your beliefs and words match your actions. Do not be accused of being a hypocrite. For people of faith who are familiar with the Bible, citing readings or specific scripture is a good strategy to point out where truth is present. You will then make some inroads with those you come into contact with on a regular basis.

Is it normal to have doubts or to question your faith?

Yes, this happens often even with the most devote and faithful. Mother Teresa in her final years expressed some doubts, and John the Baptist and others throughout scripture have had moments when they questioned their faith. This happens when people feel that their prayers haven't been answered or that God has forgotten them. Due to our self-centeredness, this can happen more than you think.

When we have doubts, it is human and not unusual. However, when we have doubts, that is when it is time to look at what we really want and why? Also, did the Lord close a window and open a door for us. In this case, "hindsight" is definitely better than foresight. In a case such as this, it is best to evaluate and reflect where we are and thank the Lord for his blessings. He may have other plans for us, or he may want you to try harder or better open your eyes to what you want before it is granted.

CHAPTER 9

How do I respond to the resurrection and hope?
The resurrection is a fundamental belief in Christianity. Without the resurrected Christ, there is no Christianity and no hope. The resurrection separates Christianity from other religions. The resurrection gives us hope that there is a second chance and that all of us can be saved.

There are times that we wonder how this could have happened. Those without faith cannot grasp the significance and the importance of Christ rising from the dead! In our daily lives, there are many opportunities for us to be enlightened, to open our eyes, and to make sense of our own status.

When we wonder how the world could be full of so many bad things, we have hope when we realize that Christ died for us, and we gain strength from his rising.

How do we gain peace?

Peace is a feeling of calm, contentment, comfort, warmth, rest, and fulfillment. Is it really possible to experience all of these at the same time? This is difficult to imagine because we as humans have anxieties, fears, needs, wants, and weaknesses. However, through our belief in Jesus Christ and the Holy Spirit, we can experience "true" peace. Our goal should be to experience "true" peace all the time. Even in the best of circumstances, this is difficult. Too many of life's issues interfere.

To answer the question, "Can true peace ever be experienced?" The answer is yes. Will it be experienced 100 percent of the time? the answer is no! When we experience "true" peace, it is through belief in Jesus Christ, prayer, meditation, and service to the Lord.

There are times when we will not be at peace. Sometimes, this is out of necessity for survival; sometimes, it is due to human turmoil and emotion. However, when we persistently and actively seek peace, it will be granted. As one of the beatitudes reads, "Blessed are those who mourn for they will be comforted."

CHAPTER 10

Free Will and the Impact on Others

In this world, the Lord has given us the opportunity for "free will," the ability to choose our destiny. Many people choose to follow the Lord, while many others do not. Unfortunately, this "free will" allows people to violate the teachings of the Lord, commit crimes in society, and hurt other people.

Take a moment to think about the responsibility this places on each individual! If someone chooses to follow the Lord, this usually is never 100 percent. People make mistakes and use their "free will" sometimes in opposition to Christian teachings. When this occurs, it may have a negative impact on others or ourselves. It is therefore best to work hard to use our "free will" appropriately and to repent and ask the Lord for forgiveness when we do not.

Others and the Impact of Their "Free Will" on Us

What other people do affects us! We live in a world where we interact with people all the time. Sometimes, they do things that interfere with our daily lives, sometimes intentionally and sometimes unintentionally. For example, while driving, someone cuts you off. In the supermarket, you have to wait in line a long time because someone has a great number of coupons. Someone spills nails in the road causing drivers to get flat tires and cause accidents. Parents abuse their children who then have academic and behavioral problems at school that interferes with other children. Someone is prejudiced, and they randomly attack people who look a certain way.

Each and every one of these instances could affect us as individuals. It is therefore best that we stay vigilant in our faith so that we can best cope when one of these occurs. Also, this prepares us to see our Lord during these difficult times.

CHAPTER 11

Do Christians have to be pacifists, quiet, and accepting at all times? The answer to this is no! Christians are called to be good people. They are called to love thy neighbor, obey the Ten Commandments, serve the Lord, and do good deeds. However, this does not mean to sit silently as others abuse power, bully others, and force us to abandon our beliefs.

Jesus was not always calm and passive. In fact, he was just the opposite. He was brought into this world to stir things up, to upset the "status quo." There were times when he was angry with people (in the temple with the money changers), disappointed in people (Peter and the other apostles when they wouldn't wait up with him the night before his arrest), and assertive (when he chose to meet with the tax collectors and prostitutes), contrary to what the priests believed should happen. Jesus shook things up! He proclaimed the truth and the way to all, just not those loyal temple attendees.

To Jesus, all were welcome to the Lord's table.

How do I proclaim the mysteries of our faith?

As Christians, our beliefs are rooted in mysteries that cannot be proved or disapproved by science. It is our role to proclaim and explain these mysteries.

Some of the more common mysteries we struggle to explain are virgin birth, (3 in 1) Father-Son-Holy Spirit, resurrection of Christ, and, if you are Catholic, the consecration of the Eucharist.

When discussing these mysteries with others, it is first important that you believe in these yourself. If you question these mysteries, then it is best to try not to explain them but to acknowledge that these are essential to the Christian faith. When you are solid in your beliefs, then it is important to explain these in simple terms and face value.

- Virgin Birth: God interceded and through the Holy Spirit impregnated Mary
- Father-Son-Holy Spirit: God, Jesus, and the Holy Spirit are united as one
- Resurrection of Christ: Christ rose from the dead on the third day
- Consecration of the Eucharist: simple bread and wine through the Eucharistic prayer and the intercession of the Holy Spirit, turn the bread and wine into the essence of Jesus Christ

Depend on your faith and their faith, no further explanation is necessary.

How do we explain creation to others?

This can be a challenge! People who believe in science and evolution only, have a hard time with the explanation in the Bible. Likewise, people who are agnostics or atheists also have a hard time with the explanation in the Bible.

People of other faiths and religions have a creation belief that in some ways are similar to the one in the Bible, so they may be more open to what the Bible says. Regardless of whom we are speaking to, it is important to emphasize that life cannot start from nothing. The Lord had to initiate life. Throughout history, historians, philosophers, scientists, and religious writers have documented and proposed logically and spiritually how life began. Of course, people for personal reasons have chosen to believe one of these over the other.

In total, the bottom line is as St. Thomas Aquinas argued, that the Lord is and ever shall be; therefore, life had to come from somewhere and that is the Lord. If evolution or adaptation to one's environment has occurred, it is a part of the Lord's master plan.

Why has the Lord allowed for the development of so many religions?

This question is difficult to answer. However, think for a minute about "free will." The Lord gives us "free will"; therefore, we have a choice what to believe. Of course, many people have only been exposed to only one religion or none at all. What about them? In some cases, the Holy Spirit will intervene and touch their heart, giving them what they need. In other cases, the Lord will expose people to some form of religion with at least some universal beliefs of right and wrong. This will enable people to live a life that can be touched by the Holy Spirit, which seeks us out even when we may not be seeking it.

CHAPTER 12

Shall the Bible text be interpreted literally or contextually as a whole? This debate has been going on for centuries, so let us "bury the hatchet" here. Put aside the argument and instead look at the essence of truth and wisdom that we encounter and absorb as we read, study, and meditate on the readings in the Bible.

Let us concentrate on the basic truths we read and move on from there. After all, we have much more in common with the fundamental beliefs of Christianity than we do with our differences. We believe in Jesus Christ, we believe in the virgin birth, we believe in the resurrection of Jesus Christ, we believe that he said to love your neighbor, we believe that he wants us to repent as sinners, and there are many more beliefs we have in common.

Consequently, there is more than one way to interpret the Bible, individually, as a group, as a church community, literally, holistically, and even in a political or historical perspective. Rather than fighting over these, it is best to focus on the fundamental areas in which we agree.

What about readings and books that have been left out of certain versions of the Bible?

As you know, the Bible is a compilation of books and readings from a number of people throughout the history of Judaism and Christianity. Not all Bibles have the same readings or books in them. Both the Old Testament and New Testament can include some different information depending on the specific denomination or sect of the group that published it. Though these differences are not always major, they reflect a study of the readings and books over history with reflection and debate.

So whose version is correct? Actually, all of them contain the basic truths and beliefs of the Jewish and Christian faiths. They differ in ways that do not invalidate the basic truths of our beliefs as Christians. Again, we should focus on what we agree on, and we should be curious as to what each other include and why.

This will give us a better understanding as to where others may be coming from. This will also better help us to confirm not only our own beliefs, but give us insight into the basic beliefs of others.

What about those who treat the Bible as a historical record and nothing more?

My first response is, "Did they actually read it?" For nonbelievers, the Bible may be just another history book. However, I challenge anyone to read the Bible from cover to cover and still believe that it is only a history book. There are many truths and much wisdom included, but to garner this requires thorough reading, meditation, and, if you are not a believer, then an open mind.

When you read statements parables and quotes from Jesus, you can't help but to actually feel the light go on as you "Get it." You understand and feel the word. Look at the Beatitudes, for example, they are full of wisdom that you can actually feel. Especially if you have experienced one of the Beatitudes. Look at the parable of the Prodigal Son. How about the Good Samaritan? These parables are full of truths and relevant throughout all time periods. Yes, the Bible is historical, but it is much, much more!!

CHAPTER 13

What does the afterlife mean to different religions?

The "afterlife'" is viewed differently by different religions for many reasons. The focus for Christians is to communicate our view and why. It is not our role to refute what others believe, but rather to educate them as to what our belief is as Christians.

Yes, we believe in the "afterlife!" Yes, we believe in the resurrection of the body when the Lord ends this world! Yes, we believe in our soul leaving the body after death and joining the father through our belief in Jesus Christ.

Some religions believe there is no "afterlife" and that we should strive to make heaven on earth by staying connected to God. Others believe that we get reincarnated and continue on in the "circle of life." Still others believe that "what is" is "what is," and there is nothing more! Therefore, we must strive to educate others to what our belief is as Christians.

What about the devil and the "afterlife?"

Some people doubt the existence of the devil. Some people believe all things have natural causes with no relation to the acts of the devil. However, when you see the evil and hatred that has been espoused throughout history, and actual worship of the devil by certain sects, it becomes apparent that the devil is a real force. Some believe he is the bad side of your conscience; others believe he is an actual force that entices, challenges, and encourages you.

As Christians, we believe the devil is an evil force that is vying for our souls. This force masks itself by enticing our senses and playing with our emotions. That is why it is important to practice restraint and moderation when tempted by something that is contrary to our beliefs.

If you are someone that does not believe in the evil force of the devil, then try to focus on the laws of your society or of what your community believes to be right or wrong. Every time you do something that violates the tenants of Christianity or, instead, in general do something wrong, the devil wins.

If the devil continues to win, then you are looking at present a separation from God and in the long run (afterlife), a permanent separation from God. If you are a nonbeliever, you may not always be separated from God. (You may be in God's grace for good deeds or spiritual connection through the Holy Spirit.) Therefore, do not take the risk of separation, temporarily or permanently.

Yes, the devil is an evil force in this world, be on the lookout.

CHAPTER 14

What is the status of "Church vs. state," worldwide?
The answer to this is quite clear. It is as varied as the nations of the earth. In some countries, there exists a theocracy, religious-based government; in others, they are totally secular, and then there are those that are atheistic (communism). Here in the United States, we have a government that is based on Judeo-Christian values, but it is mostly secular.

The "Establishment Clause," in the U.S. Constitution, prohibits the establishment of a religion, but guarantees the free exercise therewith. Our form of government gives us the right to freedom of worship, without government interference, and at the same time, it offers support to religious groups in limited ways. For example, students that attend private religious schools are entitled to receive Federal Title I education funding. Also, some faith-based organizations receive federal money who assist them with their missions.

In countries where a theocracy exists or an atheistic government exists, people do not have the freedoms to worship as Christians as we do here in the United States.

Why do we as Christians evangelize? Are we pushing our views on other cultures?

When the Lord calls, we should say, "Send me!" In our society, evangelizing is common. We as Christians are obligated to let our faith shine. Our faith should not be hidden under a rock, but rather shone like a light for all to see. When we evangelize, we should be respectful of other religions and cultures, and we must not cause harm or damage to those we evangelize. Rather, we should through our actions and words proclaim and display the spiritual richness and beauty of our beliefs. Our actions alone and our daily discussions of the truth should show the way and display the light for others. This can be demonstrated through simple acts of kindness and everyday conversations of encouragement. We cannot force belief, only nurture it.

CHAPTER 15

Why does the Lord hide from us? Or does he?

A common question I hear is, "Why does the Lord not appear to us physically and perform miracles in front of us?" Also, I hear, "If the Lord exists and cares, why doesn't he show himself?"

Well, the answer is in the scriptures when we are told not to put the Lord to the test. This was also very clear when Jesus rebukes the devil when the devil challenges him to perform miracles while in the desert for forty days and nights. Also, we are told that the Lord is pleased when we do not see and still believe unlike his disciple Thomas, who believed only when seeing the resurrected Jesus.

To the contrary of the statement that the Lord does not show himself or perform miracles, we do actually see the Lord and see him perform miracles every day! Our problem is that we sometimes do not slow down enough to appreciate the signs we are given.

To see the Lord, look around you. View the smells, sounds, and beauty of nature. See the good deeds going on around you where people are helping people. Despite some setbacks, think of the blessings you and others around you have received.

To view the miracles of the Lord, think about the good things or positive surprises that have changed your life or those around you for the better.

The Lord speaks to us and shows us the path in many ways.

His message may come through other people, circumstances, or opportunities. His miracles may come through these same mediums. The Lord knows us better than we know ourselves, and he will reach out to touch us in ways that we do not understand. Oftentimes, when we are in some type of need, the Lord talks to us, touches us, heals us, and pardons us. Sometimes, this occurs when we pray and others when we are in our time of deepest doubt.

For example, you may be in doubt of the Lord because you just found out that you lost your job and you are in desperate need of money. However, in due time, you get a job where you are happier and overall better off. In another case, someone close to you has been in bad health and eventually dies, and you question the Lord. In time, the Lord grants you peace in knowing they are no longer suffering.

Even for those that doubt and do not believe, the Lord knocks on their door. He is always calling, We just have to listen. To see the Lord and his miracles, one only needs to open their heart and eyes, and the Lord will be there holding your hand and lifting you up! He does not cure us, he does not solve all of our problems, and he does not change the world order for us. Instead, he comforts us, he heals us, he inspires us, he opens our eyes to see what has been in front of us the whole time, and, yes, sometimes, he humbles us to help us realize he is there.

CHAPTER 16

Is it okay for Christians to be wealthy?
This question is often asked, and the answer varies depending on who you speak with. To be succinct, there is nothing in the scripture that states that being rich is a sin; however, the Lord asks us to not take advantage of others to get rich. Additionally, if one is rich, it is important, since you have been blessed, to assist those in need.

When Jesus was seeking followers, he asked that people give up everything to follow him. This was especially true of the rich man who asked what it would take to follow Jesus. He asks that we give up everything in the sense that we cannot have two masters. So it is important to note that it is okay to be rich as long as the wealth does not become our master to us over him.

Is tithing necessary?

Tithing is our way of giving back to the Lord for our blessings. Money is not the main object here, but the fact that we are giving for a higher cause. We give to help the church so it can continue its good deeds, and we give so that others may benefit. Sometimes, these others are less fortunate than us, and other times, the giving benefits the larger group including us (such as a church building program or paying for religious education director). The Lord does not judge us for how much we give, but rather the genuine intent and reasons behind our giving. Therefore, be generous, but give what you can afford to give without neglecting yourself or your family.

CHAPTER 17

Baptism, infantile, or adult? Full submergence or pouring of water with anointing of oil?

There are those who support one form of baptism over another. When it comes down to it, only the baptism should matter, not when it is done. Infantile baptism is believed to initiate the child into the Christian community (as the Jewish people did with circumcision) and take away original sin. Then later in life through an altar call or the sacrament of confirmation, one consciously and willfully commits oneself to Jesus. On the other hand, with adult baptism (as early Christians did), one consciously decides to accept Jesus as an adult with full knowledge and commitment. By some, it is believed original sin is also cleansed at this time.

Some religions and Christian denominations believe in "full immersion" in the water as John the Baptist did, while others believe in pouring water on the head and then anointing the head with oil as was done in some early church traditions. Regardless of how your church or denomination does this, the bottom line is that baptism is a good thing. It is a connection to God, and it is a commitment to Jesus and your Christian community. We should support and encourage baptism and welcome all new Christians regardless as to how they were baptized as long as they show and live their commitment.

CHAPTER 18

We hear about scandals with religious groups, are they corrupt?
Like all human organizations, religious groups and individuals in those groups can take advantage of their situation to push their own personal agenda. Usually when this occurs, it is because of lack of oversight and internal controls. Just because someone is of the faith, it doesn't mean they are perfect. Therefore, it is first and foremost important to accept that, from time to time, people in religious groups are corruptible. In some cases, even entire groups or organizations can become corruptible.

What does corrupt look like?

Corruption can take many forms. However, it becomes obvious when people or organizations put their interests before those they serve. This occurs when people embezzle money. It occurs when they abuse or neglect children. This occurs when they make decisions and then hide them from the congregation or group. This occurs when they mislead or lie to the congregation or group to advance a private agenda.

When some of these things happen, you have a problem.

What to do?

When we become aware of an individual or a group/organization that is demonstrating that it has corrupt elements, it is our duty to follow the proper channels to address it. If it involves legal issues, it should be brought to the authorities. If the issues are domestic, then the governing body or if necessary the entire congregation need to be made aware of the situation. Your actions will uphold the integrity of your congregation/organization. After all, we are here to serve the Lord, not the desires of men.

CHAPTER 19

What causes people to behave the way they do? Nature or nurture?
This debate has been going on throughout the history of man. In summary, it appears after looking at all of the research that has taken place, both nature and nurture play a part in the development of a person's personality. Studies with identical twins exposed to different environments showed similar personalities, while identical twins exposed to the same environment showed different personalities. Therefore, it is reasonable to assume that not all variables can be controlled and that human development is very complex. With this in mind, we as Christians need to provide a healthy and safe environment to our youth to reduce the chances of someone becoming dysfunctional or having social and psychological issues. We will never eliminate these problems, but we can maximize the positive development of our youth.

How do we know if someone has true intentions as a Christian or is just going along?

The answer is faith! If a person has true faith, then their behavior will reflect this faith. For instance, if someone purports to be a true Christian and they are not welcoming to visitors or they do not give time, talent, prayer, or support to the congregation and others, then they may only be going through the motions. If someone is just going through the motions, it is reasonable for us to try to get them more involved. Invite them to participate in various activities and ministries. People are interested, but oftentimes, they need to be invited. You will be surprised by their responses.

CHAPTER 20

The Theories of Chaos and Random Occurrences

These theories exist and play a part in our everyday lives. Basically, these theories outline the fact that things sometimes happen by accident, they are not planned, they are random. This can sometimes explain why bad things happen to good people or innocent people are at the wrong place at the wrong time. Although there is an organization to the earth and the universe as constructed by God, it is explained by theories and laws developed by man. In other words, we cannot always predict everything, especially cause and effect.

Two good examples of the Chaos Theory or Random Occurrences are people driving cars or walking through a busy subway station. There are rules and regulations both written and unwritten that people are expected to follow. (Stay on your side of the road, or let passengers off the subway before you enter the car.) However, people react emotionally, have accidents, do not pay attention, are self-centered in their point of view, and are flat-out defiant. Consequently, where there should be organization, there is chaos or randomness.

The order of the universe as created by God, and the teachings of our Lord help us to reduce this chaos and randomness by giving us guidance and a common understanding. The Lord does not always intervene on our behalf as individuals, he gives us free choice. When Jesus knew his friend Lazarus was sick and dying, he did not intervene immediately as Mary and Elizabeth requested. He even wept when Lazarus died. However, he did finally intervene when he felt it was appropriate, so too with us.

Keeping this in mind, it is important for us to follow the word and try not to falter, since with this comes randomness and chaos.

CHAPTER 21

How do I explain Christianity to someone who has never been exposed to it?

This though difficult can be done and done well. To begin with, it is important to assess what that person may already know or doesn't know about Christianity. To start, you may want to ask them to explain to you what they know about Christianity. This will give you an excellent starting point. Begin with the Old Testament and Judaism. Focus on these topics:

- Creation/Garden of Eden/the Great Flood
- Moses Escape out of Egypt
- Burning Bush/Ten Commandments
- Some of the Prophets
- The Prophecy of the Messiah
- The Virgin Birth/Christmas
- The Youth of Jesus
- John the Baptist/Baptism of Jesus
- Jesus and the Twelve Apostles/Travels and Teaching
- The Passion/Holy Week and Easter
- The Resurrection/the Mysteries of Faith
- The Acts of the Apostles
- Early Christians/Holy Roman Empire
- Dark Ages/Monasteries
- Protestant Reformation
- Modern-Day Christian Churches

Throughout your teachings, always ask if there are questions or confusion. Then give examples of how Christians implement and practice their beliefs every day.

CHAPTER 22

Suffering and Healing

In our world, there is much pain and suffering. However, there is a great deal of healing. People are in pain, people suffer, and people are brutalized. All of this happens because of randomness and the free will of the human race. Sometimes, the Lord intervenes, and sometimes he does not. Why? We do not know for sure, but for those who seek healing and comfort, they receive it regardless of the circumstances they are going through. The healing and the peace are a feeling of the presence of the Lord. A feeling of warmth and companionship with his presence. This is reassurance that no matter what you are going through, in the end, all will be okay with the Lord.

Sometimes, we feel abandoned because our pain and suffering are not always cured. However, the key is the peace and comfort we receive when we are suffering.

How do we assist those who are suffering?

The best thing we can do is to pray for them and to provide whatever kind of support they need. Most people more than anything appreciate the fact that you are thinking of them. The support can be long term or short term. It depends on their level of need. The most important thing is to be present; other things are important, but this is at the top of the list.

How do you know if someone is healed?

This is sometimes difficult to assess. However, you can get a general idea by the outlook, attitude, and overall appearance of a person. Remember, healing is not curing, it is a state of feeling, of peace, of comfort, of enlightenment. When someone is healed, they have been heard by the Lord, and they know it. This results in them being accepted by the Lord and comforted by the Lord.

CHAPTER 23

What is important to Christians?

There are many things that Christians value and feel are important. First and foremost, it is the acceptance of Jesus Christ as our savior. Throughout history, there have been ups and downs with the church. However, the church has survived for thousands of years. To Christians, living a good life is important while staying connected to the Lord. As Christians, it is important that we behave in a Christ-like way and that we act as good role models for our faith. This means that we just do not say we believe certain things, but we actually demonstrate our beliefs. If we purport to love our fellow man and to forgive, then we need to forgive our neighbor when he does us wrong. We need to love a person even if we do not like them. This means to treat them with human dignity and respect and to help them when in need even if we do not like them.

Is our work and profession a ministry?

Yes, absolutely our work is a ministry. Everything we do as Christians is a ministry. We cannot turn Christianity on and off. We know that certain settings do not allow us to openly preach or promote Christianity; however, by our actions and our words, we can still be a "whole" Christian regardless of setting. Always put your best foot forward and stand for what is right by Christ and do not let the environment, culture, or setting in which you work dictate your Christianity. Some professions have certain mind-sets or cultural beliefs that dictate behavior. Do not let these influence your actions and words. For example, if you work in a retail establishment and it is common and acceptable among peers to steal from the establishment, do you steal or maintain your Christian values?

Family Values

This term is used often and means many things to many people. To us, family values means exactly what it says, "valuing the family!" In our busy world of today, sometimes, the family takes a backseat to many other things. However, in a Christian family, family comes first. When considering family values, it is important to see the family as an extension of the faith. All actions, words, and thoughts should be based on the teachings of the Christian faith. Children should see parents as witnesses to the faith and should be exposed to all facets of the faith. It is not acceptable to preach one thing and do another!

Interactions with Others

Positive and appropriate interactions with others are important to Christians. First and foremost, we must lead and inspire through our actions. If people know we are Christians and we do not act like a Christian would, then they will view us as hypocrites. If they do not know we are Christians, and we do not behave appropriately, then they sure are not going to want to be like us. Case in point: one of our friends in the past has been well-off with a bit of a superior attitude. They suddenly lose their job and they come to us for help. We judge them based on their attitude and deny the help. Another case: someone of a different faith visits our church out of curiosity. We do not welcome them because we have some scriptural differences of opinion. Does this reflect our Christian faith?

Does this mean we are to be nice all the time and passive?

The answer to this is no! As Christians, we are also human. We get angry, opinionated, resentful, jealous, and emotional. However, to best reflect our beliefs, we need to control ourselves as much as possible and love our neighbor. When we see injustice or evil, we must also speak out. If someone is behaving in an abusive way to others, or violating the laws of the Lord, then we need to not be passive observers, but to speak out! Speaking out can be done individually or as a group. This can be done through social media, radio, TV, newspapers, demonstrating, and just simply voicing one's opinion and challenging the behavior of groups or individuals.

How do we deal with inappropriate TV shows, radio, social media, and the media in general?

First of all, we cannot take on the world. However, we can focus on one or two items. The first item is to get our own house in order. If there are TV shows that are too violent or full of inappropriate language and inappropriate behavior, then we need not watch them. We should do the same with social media sites, publications, and radio stations.

The second thing we should do when given the opportunity is let these mediums know you are not using them and why. This will send them and their advertisers a strong message.

The third thing we should do is promote healthy mediums, sites, publications, and advertisers that support them. This can be done by word of mouth and by the very mediums that we use every day.

Will we be able to eliminate all of the inappropriate media that is contrary to our beliefs? The answer is no! However, we can influence many in a positive way to perhaps add or change programming that is closer to our Christian Faith.

In such a world that we live in, how do we protect our children from these messages that are contrary to our beliefs?

The best protection is a good solid Christian upbringing. Of course, this alone will not protect children from bad influences. However, it will arm them with what they need to resist temptation and to know better which is right and which is wrong. This upbringing involves us as the parents being the first and foremost source of education. Then good and consistent education through your church or congregation reinforces your teachings. We also need to give children some leeway and the space to make judgments and to make mistakes. This is how they learn to cope and to measure their responses to the world around them while maintaining their beliefs.

CHAPTER 24

What shakes people out of their complacency?

This is a question we all ask from time to time. Normally a life-changing event, an inconvenience, or significant change in one's routine result in a "call to action." Therefore, to get someone to make a commitment, or to take a "leap of faith," it is important to guide them into a life-changing situation.

For example, if we want someone to make a commitment to get baptized or to partake in a sacrament, we must emphasize the urgency of the commitment. Perhaps emphasize how they will be a good role model for others. Maybe even emphasize that time is of the essence so that they will be positioned to help others. Some tragic event may have even happened in their life where we can emphasize how important this commitment will be in coping with this tragedy. Whatever methods we use should be supportive and incremental.

With the Bible and clergyman preaching the word, what causes this complacency among men?

People are a stubborn lot. Just as the "rich man," who would not help the starving Lazarus who was sitting outside his gate, we do not listen to Moses, the prophets, and Jesus Christ! Like Thomas, we sometimes want to see proof before we believe. The best way to address this is by incorporating our faith into all we do. If people see us witnessing, this betters the chances that they will also. People get preoccupied with the day-to-day issues of life and seldom pause to smell a beautiful rose that they may pass by. Therefore, it is essential that we pause to see the beauty in every day. Most of the time, it is right in front of our eyes. Take a moment to notice it. It could be the smile of a friend, a compliment you gave or received, the clear blue sky, a pretty cardinal that landed nearby, a child exploring the back-yard, or a great cup of coffee! Whatever it might be, take the time to notice, appreciate, and thank the Lord for that moment. It will refresh your spirit and your day. This will snap us and others out of complacency and into appreciation!

What is the difference between knowing better and doing better?

To know better and not do better is a good example of complacency. Many of us know what the Lord teaches and we truly believe it. However, we have difficulty in implementing it day by day; in other words, we know what we should be doing and we believe it is right by the Lord, but we do not do it.

This is sometimes called "cognitive dissonance!" This happens because we get caught up in human emotions and pettiness. When we feel this occurring or know it is occurring, then it is time to slow down and think about what we are doing and why. For instance, we know it is wrong to judge others, but we do it daily. By simply meditating on these actions, and deliberately working to improve them, we can better improve our behavior.

CHAPTER 25

How does the Holy Spirit work?

This is left to faith. The Holy Spirit is there for us. The Lord offers it to us as a "gift of gifts!" We receive the Holy Spirit when we are baptized. We also receive it when we experience the sacraments. The Holy Spirit gives us many gifts such as strength, wisdom, courage, confidence, awareness, empathy, forgiveness, the ability to forgive, fortitude, foresight, intuition, love, understanding, and many more. The gifts of the Holy Spirit are sometimes given when prayed for, sometimes given when the Lord deems necessary, and sometimes with us all of the time and only realized when we are in a time of need. These gifts of the Holy Spirit are something that the Lord provides to us as we deal with the ups and downs of life. Let us say that when we receive the gift of the Holy Spirit, we in a way become capable of things that we would have never thought we can do.

Why are the gifts of the Holy Spirit oftentimes not given the attention they deserve?

When reading the Acts of the Apostles, one can see the true scope of the Holy Spirit. In this section of the Bible, it is not under-represented. Oftentimes, we focus on the life of Christ and all he did. Although the Holy Spirit is mentioned often by Christ, we do not focus on it as much as we do on him. When Christ is resurrected and the apostles become empowered by the "tongues of fire" with the Holy spirit during Pentecost, to spread the word, we see what the Holy Spirit enables them to do. This inspires us. It shows us what we may also be capable of in our daily lives. Do not underestimate the

Holy spirit, but rather pray and mediate on what it can enable us to do.

Is the Holy Spirit one and the same as God?

If we believe in the "Father and of the Son and of the Holy Spirit," then yes, the Holy Spirit is one and the same as God. This is one of the "mysteries of our faith." When the Lord sends the Holy Spirit to us, or we call on the Holy Spirit, we are being touched by the Lord. When people reached out to touch Jesus to be healed, they touched the Lord. We can do the same through our contact with the Holy Spirit.

How long does the Holy Spirit stay with someone?

As long as you stay in touch with the Lord through prayer and meditation, you will have access to the Holy Spirit. This contact can involve the Holy Spirit if one is seeking it or those who are granted it based on the circumstances. The bottom line is, "Stay in contact with the Lord." This will enhance your involvement with the Holy Spirit.

CHAPTER 26

How does evil manifest itself in the world?

This happens every day, and it can happen in many ways. Most of the time, it manifests itself through violence. Evil for the most part influences people to degrade human life, especially for those that are not like them. There are many scientific and clinical explanations and definitions for this evil; however, the main source is the "free will" of man to follow the devil. When a person becomes vulnerable for whatever reason, the devil is there to exploit and take advantage. Also, when we become greedy, self-centered, arrogant, and stiff necked as the Jewish people did when fleeing Egypt, we become an easy target. Therefore, it is important for us to remain vigilant and attentive to our beliefs and how we are behaving at all times.

What is the difference between deliberately acting evil and accidently doing something that is evil?

There is a difference. It is a matter of conscience. When we do something that we know is wrong and do it willfully and with intent, this is a sin. We have gone against the Lord and our conscience if we have a healthy conscience. However, when we do something that ends up being wrong, without our intent or our knowledge, then the Lord understands. Even if our actions wrong someone, the Lord looks at our honest intent. An example of this is an automobile accident or a work accident that we did not intend and could not prevent. Therefore, it is best for us to make an active effort to deliberately resist the lure of evil through staying in touch with the Lord in as many ways as possible (prayer, meditation, church attendance, good deeds daily, tithing, volunteer work, etc.).

What about angels?

Do angels really exist? Yes, they do. Throughout the Bible, angels appear to give messages from the Lord. Sometimes, these appearances are in dreams, and other times, they visibly appear. These messages from angels are an essential element of our Christian beliefs.

In recent history, there have been books written and accounts given of how angels have intervened in the lives of everyday people. These angels can appear in many forms. Sometimes, they are beings that we can really see; other times, they are interventions by those we cannot see, but know they are there. Oftentimes, they appear through the intervention of other people. Regardless of how they appear and for what reason, angels are real, and they can and will sometimes intervene in our lives.

What about the saints?

The saints are people that have risen against all odds with the intervention of the Holy Spirit. The life of a saint is extremely difficult. In all cases, they have been called by the Lord and empowered by the Lord to carry out his works in our everyday world. Our everyday world, of course, resists the actions of the saint every step of the way.

Saints are most often called by the Lord for a specific purpose or ministry. For example, citing two modern-day saints, Mother Teresa of Calcutta was called to serve the poor and bring attention to their plight, while Pope John Paul II brought unification and Christianity back to the former Soviet bloc countries. The world generally opposes saints since they challenge the established order and bring attention to things we would rather not see.

However, if it weren't for Saints, the works of the Lord may stay unnoticed and unaccomplished. Thank God for the saints who continue to complete his work on earth and give visual and substantial visibility to his works.

What about heaven?

In reference to heaven, two questions come to mind. Where is heaven and who gets there? Throughout history, the Judeo-Christian view of heaven has been portrayed in different ways. Some see it as paradise after death, others as paradise after our dead bodies are resurrected. Still, others see it as a close and loving relationship with the Lord while we are on the earth. Regardless, heaven is generally believed to be eternal peace and joy in the presence of the Lord.

In determining who gets there, the job is entirely up to the Lord. When judgment day comes, the Lord will separate the sheep and the rams as well as the weeds and the wheat. The "bottom line" is that Jesus says he is the way and that we go through him to join the Father. When our time comes, the only judge is the Lord, not us, not our clergyman, not the norms of society, but only the Lord. Therefore, it is contingent on us not to have preconceived ideas about who qualifies and who does not while we judge ourselves to be better candidates than others.

How do we know what to do to qualify for heaven?

There is no real answer to this question. Only the Lord knows. However, if we follow the words and teachings of Jesus, the Ten Commandments, and we stay in close contact with the Lord, our chances are very good.

What are some specific things we can do?

The list varies depending on who you speak. However, there are some common themes among pastors and different Christian denominations. Listed below are some actions we can take:

- Give alms to the poor
- Pray to our Lord Jesus Christ and follow his words
- Volunteer and give service to your church and community
- Tithe
- Forgive
- To ask for forgiveness
- Evangelize
- Love your neighbor and your enemy

Any of these actions will enhance our chances of attaining heaven.

How should we pray?

Praying can be done as a group in church, a prayer group, or a family. It can also be done individually. In church or in a prayer group, it is usually a common prayer that everyone says together.

Individually, it can be a prayer developed by a church or religious group for a special purpose, or it can be whatever you want to say to the Lord. The most important thing is that you are communicating with the Lord, staying in touch, and showing your reverence. Praying as a group gives power to the prayer and confidence to the group since it has group support behind it. Prayer also gives a feeling of peace, comfort, and satisfaction to the group and individual. Pray as often as you can. You will feel better, and you will feel the presence of the Lord.

CHAPTER 27

What is the future of the Christian church?
    This is a very often asked question. In Europe, church attendance is way down, and some claim it is a "post-Christian era" in Europe. In the United States, church attendance is still quite high, especially in the South, but declining. However, some groups in the Christian church heavily evangelize and are slowly growing. Additionally, Pope Francis is making efforts to keep and attract more people to the faith through reforms and outreach. In other parts of the world, Christians are being persecuted and are fleeing in high numbers to countries more tolerant of religious freedom. Consequently, the future of the Christian church appears to be in jeopardy.

What can we do?

We as Christians have an opportunity to help. As we have discussed earlier, our best resource in spreading the faith is to be a good Christian example for others. This includes demonstrating what Christians do, not just what we believe. We cannot preach one thing and do another. Young people and people of other faiths especially will see through any hypocrisy. Additionally, we must be willing to stand up for what is right, and we must always question things that are purported as truths.

What can the Christian church do?

To start, the Church may have to increase its outreach to young people. Young people are the future of the church. The church does not have to change its beliefs or principles, but it will have to make a deliberate effort to get young people involved. The first step would be for each church to have a youth minister if they do not already have one. Secondly, during sermons, the readings should be made relevant to the lives of all people including young people. Young people have a lot of energy and good ideas and therefore should be invited to participate in committees and ministries that have a direct impact on the church. Young people should be deliberately engaged.

What do people sometimes shun organized religion?

People may shun organized religion for many reasons: an unpleasant personal experience, a lack of involvement, a lack of exposure as a child, a disagreement on doctrine, the fact that they do not fully have a deep understanding or an appreciation for the religion they have been involved in, and possibly many other reasons. Sometimes, if life is good, we feel we do not need the church or God.

Oftentimes, this shunning of organized religion is legitimate and understandable. Other times, this can be a sign of self-centeredness or the feeling that the church is not necessary in one's life. Regardless of the reason, we should make every effort to make people feel welcome and to accept them as equals. Our behavior can go a long way in helping individuals and our own churches.

How do we explain to young people how the organized church or religion comes up with its dogma or rules?

First, we must emphasize that dogma and rules are not arbitrary and capricious. The founders of particular churches and congregations have drawn on centuries of debate, discussion, research, and differences of opinion to develop their particular dogma. Starting with the Old Testament, then the unwritten early traditions of Christianity, then the New Testament and the universal church, then the Protestant Reformation, then the Great Awakening, then the emergence of more diverse Christian Churches, and finally our present-day issues, they have all contributed to what our churches have today. Christian churches of all denominations have held numerous councils, conventions, and meetings over centuries, decades, and years, to decide what they will believe and what they will not believe. This is also the case of many non-Christian religions. Therefore, it is important to note that when we join a church, we purport to believe what they believe.

CHAPTER 28

How do I choose a church?

This is a serious matter and should not be taken lightly. As we know, not all churches are the same. Some are members of large organizations, while others are small independent churches. It is our responsibility to choose the church that you are most comfortable attending and that which reflects your beliefs. It is important not to join a church and then try to alter your true beliefs to fit in unless you truly are committed to what the church stands for and believes in. This is also the case in determining your overall mission in life.

Churches vs. Prisons!

Did you ever wonder where we would be if there were not so many churches? We have enough problems as it is. Imagine if there were fewer churches. More than likely, there would be more prisons. Some people, especially those that may not participate or value organized religion, may not see the practical result of what churches do. Like other organized institutions, churches serve a very important role in our society by teaching our young people. Churches help promote the difference between right and wrong as they help build the moral fiber of a society. I always say, "The more churches, the better!"

CHAPTER 29

Why is history portrayed differently by different religious groups?
History has always been shaped by those who report it! Religious groups as historians write history based on their own beliefs, biases, and perspectives. It is our responsibility as Christians to keep this in mind when we read and hear about the differences of opinions during the Reformation. Likewise, we should do the same with the crusades. The bottom line is we must focus on the truths of our faith and view everything through this perspective. Is it right to kill people in the name of God? Is it right to mistreat someone due to their race, gender, ethnicity, religious beliefs, or other factors? These are issues we deal with every day. When in doubt, talk to your clergyman or the clergy of other faiths.

What then is our measure as a Christian?

Our measure as a Christian is to follow the words of Jesus. We must consciously and deliberately practice what Jesus taught. If our church, family, and friends go against the teachings of Christ, we need to be steadfast in our convictions.

What does history have to do with now?

History has everything to do with now. Things that we believe and that institutions promote have been shaped by history. This history is sometimes clear and righteous and other times gray and contradictory. Most religious groups and organizations have had scandals and missteps. Do not let this shade your beliefs and actions. As humans, we make up groups and institutions, and we make mistakes. Sometimes, the media will make a villain of a church or religious institution; accept this and move forward with good intentions and a commitment to the words of Jesus Christ.

Why pray?

Praying is our window to God. By praying, we are in touch with the Lord. We are communicating our regrets, sorrows, inspirations, thankfulness, good wishes for ourselves, and good wishes for others, and we ask for forgiveness. Prayer by us for others makes them stronger. Prayer for us by others makes us stronger. Prayer is not us asking the Lord for things and him granting them. Prayer is much more than this. The Lord will answer our prayer one way or another. We may get what we want either directly or in a roundabout way. We may also not get what we are asking for, but instead be enlightened concerning our situation. Prayer is good for our soul and those around us. Pray for yourself and others, and you will find comfort.

CHAPTER 30

What of Lent and Advent?

Lent and Advent are times of expectation and preparation. Advent is preparation for the birth of our Lord Jesus Christ, and Lent is the preparation for the resurrection of our Lord Jesus Christ. They are similar, yet different. They are similar in the way that we are asked to meditate, perhaps fast, to do good deeds, to perhaps sacrifice by giving something up, and to pray.

They are different in the sense that Advent is a time of joy for the coming of the Lord. On the other hand, Lent is a time of solemn anticipation of the human death of our Lord, to be followed by the joyful resurrection.

Both Lent and Advent bring us closer to the Lord and closer to an understanding of what our faith is all about.

Do all Christian faiths practice Lent the same way?

Not really. Some give it a big emphasis, and others give it a passing notice. It depends on what church you belong to. There is no right or wrong way to recognize Lent. However, the important thing to take note of is the significance of the things you do during Lent and why. If your church emphasizes Lent, then make the best of it by participating fully. If your church recognizes it in passing, then at least recognize it the terms that your church offers. The important thing is to use this opportunity to get closer to our Lord.

The Psalms!

What are the Psalms and why are they important to Christians? The Psalms date back many years and are said to have been written by King David. Also there is some discussion that King Solomon and some others may have had a part in the Psalms. The Psalms are poetic and musical prayers to our Lord. They contain much wisdom, foresight, and humbleness. In essence, they are beautiful tributes to our Lord and all he does for us. They are the part of Jewish temple, every Catholic mass, and many other Christian services. To sing or to read the Psalms is very uplifting and a window to our Lord.

The Stations of the Cross?

The stations of the cross are a way to pray and to recognize the passion of Jesus Christ. Through going to each of the fourteen stations of the cross, we pray, commemorate, mediate on, and internalize the sacrifice, suffering, and pain of Jesus as he is tortured for our sins. By going through the stations, we are reminded of what Jesus went through for us.

The Rosary?

The rosary is a way for Catholics to show reverence to Mary while praying to our Lord and Jesus Christ. Throughout the history of the Catholic church, the rosary has had a significant role in meditation and in praying for others. Oftentimes, the rosary is conducted as a service for those that have recently departed. To say the rosary is to participate in a communal prayer, asking for Mary to intercede with Jesus and our Lord on our behalf or the behalf of someone else.

Idols?

What is the significance of religious statues? It is common knowledge that Christians are not to worship idols. However, some Christian groups use idols as symbols to remind them of religious personalities. Most Christians that pray in the presence of idols do so to have the idol remind them of the entity they are praying to. For example, if someone is praying in front of a statue of Jesus, they are praying directly to Jesus with the statue there to remind them of Jesus. Sometimes, this is misunderstood. Also, statues give us a visual reminder of Our Lord, Mary, the saints, and others. This helps us to remember them and to feel close to them. Statues and idols help us to pray to our Lord.

CHAPTER 31

Human Emotion and Intellect vs. the Word of the Lord

Yes, this is an ongoing battle. People in general tend to be emotional beings. Oftentimes, we get angry, jealous, hateful, resentful, sad, depressed, and greedy. When we act on these emotions, they are very often at odds with the word of God, especially the Ten Commandments and much of what Jesus preached. It is therefore our challenge to resist the temptations of emotions and think about what the Lord would have us do. This is a difficult task, and none of us can completely succeed 100 percent of the time. It is then that we ask for forgiveness and continue to strive for 100 percent!

Why does the Lord speak to some and not others?

Does he? The Lord speaks to everyone. However, he does not always speak in the same manner. Sometimes, it is directly through a dream or an angel. Other times, it is through a sign, the words of another person, or a life-changing event. Those that seek the Lord will usually receive more awareness of his response since they are in close contact. Others may struggle to see the response since their eyes have not been opened, or they are not aware enough to hear it. Day-to-day distractions and "noise" can interfere with our contact with the Lord. All we can do is, "Seek and we shall find and knock and we shall be let in." This is a good start for hearing the Lord.

Why does the Lord select some to be messengers or to be of religious orders? What is the criteria?

The Lord chooses people based on his reasons. Most often, he selects people based on their ability to carry his cross. Most of the time, he selects unlikely candidates, those that are not of high profile. Sometimes, they are people who are questioning their own faith such as Jonah when the Lord called on him. He tried to hide from the Lord to no avail. Basically, we cannot make the Lord choose us. He will call on us in his own way and his own timeline. We will know when we are called.

Should I plan for the future or rely on the Lord?

Of course, we should communicate with the Lord and rely on the Lord. However, the Lord wants us to take initiative, to strive for ourselves and others. We owe it to ourselves and to the Lord to make the best we can of the gifts he gives us. He does not want us to bury our talents under a rock, but instead to use these God-given talents to help ourselves and others. This means it is okay for us to work hard to improve ourselves. By doing so, we are thanking the Lord for our gifts. Also, this puts us in a position to use these gifts to assist others, to make our lives and their lives better.

Therefore, we must rely on the Lord for our strength and initiative, but use these to help ourselves and others.

What about people that scoff at or "write off" our beliefs?

This is a difficult situation. It is important for us to keep in mind that sometimes people do not understand where we are coming from. People that "write us off" and judge us are oftentimes defensive about their independence. They do not want us pushing our beliefs on them. Therefore, it is critical that we lead by example and our actions rather than our words. Most people want to do good, and most people want to get along. We must help them to see that we are not out to condemn them or convert them, but just to be their friend and neighbor.

CHAPTER 32

The Beauty of Nature

The beauty of nature is a common topic among believers and non-believers. This beauty is no accident. The Lord created the universe and everything in it. The laws of nature and the chaos of nature are all part of the Lord's plan. How all types of life work together, are dependent on each other, and rely on each other is a gift for all of us. The beauty around us reminds us that all things have beauty and that the Lord has given this gift to us. When man tries to duplicate the beauty of nature, he falls short every time. Something cannot start from nothing! Therefore, it is important for us to see the wonders of the world as gifts from God and not random scientific occurrences.

Natural Disasters

Natural disasters occur all the time resulting in physical loss, damage, and deaths. Why do these things happen? Some of it is caused by man-made actions. Sometimes, we build homes in flood-plains and on cliffs, and sometimes, we start forest fires. Other times, nature does what nature does. The weather forms, and the results can sometimes be bad for humans. Our best bet is to prevent what we can by modifying our behavior, being vigilant, and praying for our protection and the protection of others.

Does the Lord intervene with little things?

Yes, he can and does. Now, the Lord may not intervene on who wins the Super Bowl; however, he may intervene in the lives of the players. He may empower them to peak performance, or he may motivate them to do their best. Additionally, he answers prayers that are unselfish and for the good of others. For example, he may intervene when you apply for a job, not hurting other people, but enabling you to do your best. Usually, the Lord matches up people with what is best for them and ultimately others. Therefore, pray to do your best, work hard toward your best, and the Lord will do the rest.

How do I know if the Lord has intervened for me?

You will! It will not make sense at first. In fact, you may think you were forgotten! You may not have received what you asked for in the manner you wanted it. However, over time, you will see how the Lord carried you rather than abandoning you as is in the story, "Footprints in the Sand." For example, someone in your family is sick and you are caring for them, you pray for their recovery, and then you get sick. Even though you are sick, the Lord helps you through the situation. At first, you feel abandoned; however, later you see how regardless of your health you get through the situation and recover with the Lord's help. Do not doubt or deny the Lord. He will come through in his own way on his timeline.

CHAPTER 33

Physical, Spiritual, and Mental Fitness

As children of the Lord, it is important for us to maintain our overall health and fitness. By doing this, we are respecting and maximizing the gifts we have been given. Remember, we all do not have equal or the same gifts, and it is important for us to appreciate what we have and to maximize our potential. (The Lord has designed us magnificently in his own way according to his own plan.) To do this, it is important that we do everything we can to maintain our physical bodies, our spiritual being, and our mental/cognitive state. This can be done by making a conscious effort to keep ourselves sharp. (Join a gym, get physical exercise, pray, read, study, and contemplate matters larger than ourselves.) By maintaining our own health and fitness, we are better positioned to do the Lord's work to service others.

What about Social Justice?

This topic has generated much discussion and is viewed differently by different religions. Even in the Christian church, there are different views on how to deal with this topic. As you know, we as individuals and church groups cannot solve the problem of inequities in society and the abuse of human rights. However, we can do our part by initiating or participating in activities and ministries that promote respect, dignity, and opportunity for all those who are in need. We can do this by participating in advocacy groups of our choice or by actually being a part of "Feet on the Ground" who service those in need. This can be done regardless of our philosophical or political beliefs. When we serve the least of our brothers, we serve Christ.

What about "New Age" Religions?

Some will say that "New Age" religions contribute to spiritual well-being and should be pursued. This may be true for some, especially those that are still searching. However, Christianity if understood and practiced contributes to spiritual well-being more than anyone ever expects. Christianity has all of the answers, all of the wisdom, and all of the peace one would want if one meditates, prays, and practices the faith. So if you are looking for answers, you do not have to look far. Reflect on what you already believe and practice your faith.

What about Yoga, Karate, Judo, Transcendental Meditation, Mysticism, etc.?

There are many methods that people use to nurture their spiritual life, and there is a debate whether they are contrary to Christian beliefs. Some people see them as just another way to relax or connect with your inner self, while others see it as perhaps worshiping someone or something other than Christ.

The important thing to keep in mind here is intent. Although there is a holistic spiritual philosophy behind some of these activities, it depends on the intent of the person involved in these activities. For example, you may take karate for the fun, fitness, fellowship, and self-defense, despite the fact that there is a spiritual component to the art of karate. Yes, you can benefit from the activity without embracing the spiritual component. This decision will have to be made by you based on your views and beliefs.

Politics and Religion

Sometimes, these can be intertwined and difficult to separate. Religious groups and organizations as many other groups can benefit by advocacy and involvement with the political process. This assures that the rights and beliefs of the religious group are protected and not discriminated against by a majority whom they may not agree with. This advocacy or involvement can take many forms such as serving on campaigns, donating money as individuals or as groups not listed as nonprofits, demonstrating, writing emails and letters, running for office, and other forms of involvement. It is imperative that, as Christians and people of faith, we let our beliefs be known and that we participate in the political process. We may not always get what we want, but we will be defending our rights to practice our faith.

Exorcism and Possession

Exorcism and possession by demons are mentioned many times in the scriptures. Does this really exist and can the spirit and mind be inhabited by the devil? The answer to this is maybe and sometimes yes. The devil can change your consciousness, and we can commit evil acts because we get into a certain frame of mind. For example, someone watches too much violence and commits violence because they have become desensitized, people hate other people and groups and commit violence against them because of this hate, people steal from others because they become used to taking from others and think nothing of it, etc. Sometimes, this can be explained by mental illness, but other times, it is just pure evil. Praying for oneself and for others who have this presence of dysfunction or evil can help to intervene. Exorcism although not accepted by many does have Biblical references and may or not be relevant. This would have to be looked at on an individual basis.

CHAPTER 34

Self-Centeredness, Sin, and Survival

Self-centeredness is necessary for survival, yet when carried too far it is a sin. To survive as an individual, it is important for people to look out for themselves and to take individual initiative to take advantage of situations to promote their continued existence. However, where this becomes a problem is when we promote our interests above and beyond survival at the expense of our Lord and others. For example, we may have a comfortable life without need for survival, and we treat people who are struggling as less deserving than us. Unlike good Christians, we may feel contempt for those who for whatever reason cannot free themselves from addictions, mental illness, or poverty. This is where the Lord calls us into action to look beyond our self-centered ways and to help others as he would want us to do. To survive is one thing, to serve the Lord through serving others is another.

Is sin always intentional?

Good question. For something to be a sin, it has to be a willful action against the wishes of our Lord. A sin can however be one of commission or omission. For example, you can intentional wrong someone or violate one of the Ten Commandments, this is commission. Perhaps instead you can leave someone in need at the side of the road as many did before the Good Samaritan came by to help, this is omission. Regardless of the motivation, we must be aware of our actions and keep in mind what our Lord teaches us before we are involved in committing sin. At all times, be diligent and act as a Christian.

Why must we ask for forgiveness?

We must because it is the right thing to do, also it is what relieves us from the burden of sin. When we commit a sin, we wrong someone else, ourselves, or the Lord. Therefore, it is necessary that we be alleviated and cleansed from our transgressions if we are truly sorry. This makes the aggrieved party feel better, and it helps us to come to terms with improving ourselves for the future. While we must ask for forgiveness, we must also be willing and able to forgive others. This will make us better Christians.

How do we define self-centeredness?

Self-centeredness is when someone is so involved with themselves that they do nothing at all in consideration of others. This often occurs without a person being aware of it, especially if they are self-sufficient, without need, and on top of their game. When we see this, it is best to help the person understand that not everyone is like them and that there are needs out there that have to be addressed. This can be done in a nonthreatening way by including the person in discussions and activities that address the needs of others.

Survival as a Christian

Surviving as a Christian is a challenge. Living as Christ would have us to live is difficult. Oftentimes, we have to behave contrary to our human emotions and condition. It is not easy to love someone who is despicable. It is not easy to forgive; it is not always easy to tithe or to go out of your way to be a do-gooder. However, we are called to do these things and to count our own blessings, even if we are experiencing difficult times ourselves. This is the beauty of being a Christian; we believe and act as role models as heroes, as a shining light for others. We survive for these reasons!

How do we repent for our sins?

Repentance is an act of humility and is necessary to be forgiven for our transgressions. Different religions and different churches within the Christian faith have their own way of teaching and initiating repentance. Generally, repentance is seen as a way of making things right with our Lord and asking for the strength not to repeat our mistakes. We repent by asking the Lord for forgiveness and also those whom we have committed transgressions against. This is done in different ways (i.e., confession and reconciliation with a priest, an altar call, a silent vigil, personal prayer, and many others). We also forgive those who have transgressed against us. This completes the circle and makes us whole. This is not easy, and it is not always our preferred action. However, it is what is necessary to follow the Lord and to have our own inner peace.

CHAPTER 35

Volunteerism

Volunteering is an excellent way to serve the church and your community. Clearly churches of every kind contribute millions of hours and millions of dollars' worth of services to our communities every year. This takes a big burden off the government, and it provides help and assistance to millions of people and organizations. To be a volunteer is to give of oneself to others. This could be to churches, individuals, or other organizations. Volunteering is a true mission in serving our Lord by serving his people. If we do not have time to volunteer, then we can donate to or support those that do provide these services. Volunteering is the ultimate form of selflessness.

Where and how do I get involved?

It is not that difficult to get involved. All churches have ministries and opportunities for volunteering. Also, many nonprofits such thrift stores, senior centers, airports, some hospitals, schools, and civic organizations will welcome you with open arms. It is best to determine what you would like to do and then contact the appropriate organization. No job is too big or too insignificant. When you volunteer to serve, you do exactly that! You will take a big step in following our Lord.

If I cannot volunteer, then what?

If we are unable to volunteer because of family or work obligations, then it is important to give those responsibilities our best efforts. We also serve the Lord by giving of ourselves 100 percent to our responsibilities. You see, it is our mission and an extension of our faith when we give our all to the Lord through performing 100 percent in what we do. (Of course, these are responsibilities that are moral and legal.) Consequently, we can serve in many, many ways.

CHAPTER 36

Addictions/Distractions

Addictions are a big issue in our world! The nature of humans leaves us susceptible to a wide variety of addictions. As victims of addiction and helpers of those that are addicted, what do we do? The first step is to recognize and admit that an addiction exists. Once this is done, it is necessary for the addicted person to be willing to fight the addiction and to accept help in fighting the addiction. If you are the addicted, there are many faith-based support groups, clinics, volunteer, and civic organizations (some associated with churches and some that are independent) that will help you. If you are helping a person with addiction, then these organizations are also good resources for you.

Addictions can be positive and negative. A positive addiction can be going for a daily walk or avoiding foods that are not healthy. A negative addiction can be drug abuse or excessive gambling. Regardless if an addiction is positive or negative, we cannot allow an addiction to take the place of having faith in our Lord. Most addictions make our bodies and minds dependent and prisoners of certain behaviors. This dependency draws us away from making a conscious decision to have faith that the Lord is here to help us. All of us should be able to enjoy our freedoms and our God-given abilities to make the most of our opportunities.

Addictions take away this freedom and oftentimes hurt those around us who love us. It is therefore important to recognize addictions when they exist and be willing to accept help and offer help.

A great place to get this help is through the variety of faith-based opportunities that exist. This will give you the support that you or a loved one need, but also the intervention of the Holy Spirit that will support and nourish the body, mind, and spirit.

Distractions

We all are so busy. We are constantly trying to balance our responsibilities, and we are constantly fighting distractions. However, sometimes, distractions can be good. A negative distraction is something that throws us off course. It disrupts our trajectory toward our goal for the day, week, or month. A good distraction from our daily scramble would be to take a few minutes to meditate, contemplate our Lord, and pray for ourselves and others. Yes, we will have to resist negative distractions and sometimes even give in to them now and then. (Sometimes, these are unavoidable and necessary responsibilities we must address.) But keep in mind, we all should work intentionally to give ourselves positive distractions. They will revitalize us and energize us!

CHAPTER 37

What Is the Difference between Acceptance and Approval?

As Christians, it is important that we accept people where they are, but this does not necessarily mean we approve of their behavior. Throughout the scriptures, Jesus accepts people where they are and reaches out to them; he evangelizes them. Those that are considered unclean, outcasts, and sinners are embraced by Jesus as he forgives them and accepts them. We should do the same. It doesn't mean we agree with their beliefs and behaviors. It is our way of showing our love as Christians and our efforts to show them our charity. We cannot force them to believe what we do, but we can take this as an opportunity to display our true faith and to evangelize through our actions. This is a rich opportunity to show our commitment to our Lord.

How do we accept those that want to hurt us?

This is not easy. To do this, we must be willing to move on. Think of it as going through an obstacle course. You will encounter those that want to stop you, hurt you, and delay you. However, as you persist forward, keep in mind the end result. When you get there, you have to put it out of your mind; you have made it regardless. If you do not make it, no worry; the Lord will offer another opportunity or pathway. Do not dwell on those that hurt you. It will drain your energy and give them continued power over you.

How do we get the Lord's approval?

This topic is debated by different groups. However, there is a common tread. The general way to gain approval from the Lord is to follow his teachings, believe in him, ask for forgiveness, forgive others, and love your neighbor. By following these basic premises, you will gain approval as a Christian. Of course, doing these things is not as easy as we may think, so we must prepare for the challenge.

What do we do when others do not accept us because of our faith?

This happens more than people think. Oftentimes, people stay away from us because they are uncomfortable around us. This occurs because of guilt on their part or a fear that they may weaken and join the faith. Other times, it is due to ignorance, lack of understanding, or outright bias. When this is the case, it is in our best interest and the best interest of others to remain low key. It is important for us to continue with our open heart and our Christian virtues regardless of how we are perceived. However, do not be aggressive or combative since this will play into their stereotype of us. Remember, the best way for us to evangelize is through our actions.

CHAPTER 38

Darkness and Light

There is a lot of symbolism and meaning attached to these two words. Oftentimes due to culture and religious beliefs, these two words are used to describe feelings, perceptions, and expectations. In the scriptures, "light" is associated with the goodness of the Lord, and "darkness" is associated with ignorance and the evil of the devil. Regardless of one's Christian affiliation, the main point here is that we are asked to shed our Christian light on others. The Lord gives us "light" (i.e., awareness, enlightenment, understanding, epiphany, and empathy). We gain these through prayer, meditation, asking for forgiveness, forgiving, and ministry. It is therefore our responsibility to share this "light," with others. Let us not bury our "light" under a rock, but let it shine for all to see!

How do we know when we are in the dark?

This is difficult to answer. Oftentimes, we are in the dark and do not realize it until we are in the light. If you have no contact with, or inner feeling for the Lord, and if you are engaged in activities that are harmful to you and others, then more than likely you are in the dark. One way to determine this for sure is to meditate on it and ask some around who you consider pious. Also, note how you stack up against what you would like to be.

Is light the ultimate goal?

Yes, it should be our goal to see the "light" and experience the "light." To understand the Lord, to realize our purpose and position in life, and to live a fulfilling and productive life, it is important for us to be in the "light." To be in the "light" is to know God and to feel his presence in everything we see and do. If we are in this state, then we are in the "light." If we are in the "light," then we are in the presence of the Lord.

How do we get into the "light?"

Getting into the "light" can be a challenge. One way to do this is to make an intentional effort to do the right thing. The right thing is to follow the teachings of our Lord. By following his teachings and praying for his gift of the Holy Spirit, we are on our way to the "light." We will be sidetracked, tested, and challenged by the forces of the world. However, if we stay focused, we will be okay!

CHAPTER 39

Justice

How should we determine what is just? Justice can be complicated. People have their own points of view on this as individuals, groups, cultures, and countries. A "rule of thumb" is to determine justice by reflecting on the "New Testament" in the Bible. As you know, there are many universal "truths" recognized by most human cultures; however, Christians go a step further with forgiveness, reconciliation, and remorseful contrition. Justice should involve atonement, punishment, forgiveness, and acceptance. Christians unlike many other groups will punish someone to atone for their wrongs, ask them to be remorseful, ultimately forgive them, and finally accept them. Forgiveness and acceptance are two of our most significant beliefs, but are hardest to actually put into practice. Jesus says, "We should forgive 77 times!" There is a secular saying that "People who are just will be treated with justice." There is much wisdom in this saying.

Why do churches differ on views of right and wrong?

Most of the differences are in their interpretation of the Bible. Some take it literally, while others interpret it as a group. However, for the most part, most churches have the same general concepts of right and wrong. This also cuts across lines of cultures and religions other than Christian. Within every religion, there are extremists who go beyond the general tenants of right and wrong. This will sometimes skew the perceptions of certain churches and religious groups.

The bottom line is that most Christian churches are more similar in their beliefs than they are different.

What is excommunication?

Excommunication is when a person is kicked out or separated from a group. Usually this occurs when a person violates the rules or norms of a religious group. Most often, this person can reconcile and rejoin if they repent and agree to follow the conditions set by the group.

Is it just when someone is excommunicated?

In most cases, religious groups have norms, rules, and standards. If someone chooses to violate these and has voluntarily joined the group, then the group is justified in excommunicating them. The individual needs to decide, *is this what I want?* Do I believe what the group believes? Once this is decided, it is then time to move forward.

Chapter 40

Summary Narrative

What is important! What is important?

In this book, we discussed many things. We discussed many thoughts, perceptions, and questions. In this process, it was possible to determine "What is important" concerning our faith. In determining this, there are many common themes and reflections to draw upon.

Our first determination of "What is important" is that we as Christians must work hard to truly believe in Christ. This is not always easy, as we saw how John the Baptist, Peter, and others throughout the scriptures struggled with this. Therefore, we must work hard at this as our first step.

Next, it is "important" for us to act as Christians. Again, this is not easy as Christ asks us to "love our neighbor," forgive others, and put the Lord first. This takes a deliberate and conscious effort every hour of every day.

According to St. Francis of Assisi, it is also important to be a good Christian "role model," as our behavior will speak louder than our words. Demonstrate to others that Christians practice what they believe. To practice our faith is ultimately what the Lord wants of us. We are not perfect and will "slip up," from time to time. However, we must continue to move forward at a steady pace, negotiating road-blocks and hardships.

So "What is important?'

To strive in a deliberate manner to be a good Christian every day!

So "What is important!"

That we are striving to be a good Christian every day in a deliberate manner!

Epilogue

Why This book?

As a former religious education teacher for twenty years, I based this book on the questions I received from my students and others. They were legitimate, conscientious questions from people who wanted to clear up confusion, mixed messages, contradictions, and doubts that they had about their faith and that of the greater Christian church.

I hope the answers given will assist others in helping them to sort out in their own minds their "faith."

Final Statement

"Faith" is a precious gift that not all people know to seek or tend to grasp or gain. Cherish your "faith" for you are blessed

About the Author

John DeCotis is a lifelong educator with over forty years of experience in private and public schools. He holds several degrees with his terminal degree being a Doctorate of Educational Leadership and Curriculum & Instruction. He and his wife Tina, a lifelong educator, have three grown children, two sons-in-law, and one grandson. As a former religious education teacher for twenty years, he based this book on the questions he received from his students and others. They were legitimate, conscientious questions from people who wanted to clear up confusion, mixed messages, contradictions, and doubts that they had about their "faith" and the greater Christian church.

We hope the answers given will assist others in helping them to sort out in their own minds their "faith."

"Faith" is a precious gift that not all people know to seek or tend to grasp or get. Cherish your "faith" for you are blessed..